To

_____

From

_____

Date

_____

Faith for Every Season

A She Laughs at the Future
Devotional Journal

Curated by Jill Albanys

Hello dear sister,

The authors of *She Laughs at the Future* have come together to create this inspiring journal designed to support you in building your faith a little more each day.

We are honored to come alongside of women that are committed to growing closer to the Lord in every season of life.

We pray you are blessed and encouraged as you find inspiration and encouragement in *Faith for Every Season*.

Faith Refined in the Fire

Jill Albanys

Have you ever noticed how life is filled with breathtaking highs—moments that make our hearts overflow with joy and gratitude? The excitement of falling in love, the wonder of watching a child take their first steps, the satisfaction of a well-earned promotion—life holds so many reasons to celebrate.

Yet, woven into the fabric of life are also seasons of sorrow. We face times of loss, disappointment, and unexpected trials that test the very foundation of our faith.

1 Peter 1:1-9 reminds us that even in these trials, God is at work. Our faith, like gold refined by fire, is being strengthened and purified. What the enemy intends for harm, God is using for our good. Every hardship we endure is an opportunity for our faith to be shaped into something even more precious.

Take a moment to reflect: What if your current trial is not meant to break you but to build you? What if, through this very season, God is deepening your trust in Him and preparing you for something greater?

In this you rejoice greatly, even though now for a little while, if necessary, you have been distressed by various trials, so that the genuineness of your faith, which is much

Journal & Reflection

1. Think of a trial you've walked through in the past. Looking back, how can you now see that your faith grew because of it?

2. In what specific ways has your faith deepened through trials—has it made you more patient, more trusting, more resilient?

3. How does what you've learned from past trials shape the way you view your current struggles?

No trial is wasted in God's hands. He is refining, strengthening, and positioning you for greater things. Keep trusting, keep believing—your faith is being made radiant.

Prayer: *Lord, I thank you that you are God, and you are the orchestrator of my life. You know everything about me, and you see where my faith is tested at times. Walk with me through the fiery trials and help me to grow in confidence in Your Word. I am asking you to turn this test into a testimony, for your praise, honor and glory. Amen.*

Spend some time in praise and worship, continuing to express gratitude toward God.

more precious than gold which is perishable, even though tested and purified by fire, may be found to result in praise and glory and honor at the revelation of Jesus Christ. ~ 1 Peter 1:6

Additional Journaling Space

Though you have not seen Him, you love Him. Though you do not now see Him, you believe in Him and rejoice with joy that is inexpressible and filled with glory, obtaining the outcome of your faith, the salvation of your souls. ~ 1 Peter 1:8-9

According to his great mercy, He has caused us to be born again to a living hope through the resurrection of Jesus Christ from the dead, to an inheritance that is imperishable, undefiled, and unfading, kept in heaven for you, ~ 1 Peter 1:3-4

Faith for Every Season

As we journey through life, it's easy to forget that every season is designed by God with purpose and intention. Whether we find ourselves in a time of joy or trial, nothing is wasted in His hands.

We often see how God moves in seasons of abundance, peace, and celebration, but it can be harder to understand His hand at work in times of heartache, sickness, or loss. Yet, as our faith deepens, we learn to trust that God is present in every season. His promises never fail, and His Spirit continually leads us. No matter where we are right now, we are never forsaken. Even in difficulty, He is guiding us beside still waters, where our souls will be restored.

No season lasts forever, but every season has purpose. God is working all things together for good, shaping us, strengthening us, and drawing us closer to Him.

There is a season (a time appointed) for everything and a time for every delight and event or purpose under heaven.
~ Ecclesiastes 3:1-8 (AMP)

Journal & Reflection

1. What season are you in right now? Is it a season of joy, peace, transition, waiting, hardship, or healing?

2. Can you recognize God's presence in this season? How has He been speaking, providing, or leading you?

3. Do you trust that this season is in God's hands? Why or why not?

4. What has this season revealed about your faith? Has it deepened your trust, stretched your patience, or drawn you into greater dependence on Him?

It was you who set all the boundaries of the earth; you made both summer and winter. ~ Psalm 74:17

5. What scriptures can you meditate on and post around your home as a reminder of God's promises in this season?

No matter what season you're in, God is with you. He is growing you, refining you, and preparing you for what's ahead. Trust His timing, rest in His promises, and embrace His purpose in this moment.

Prayer: *In all things and in all seasons of life, you are my God. In times of joy, I will praise you, in times of struggle, I will trust you. You are my Strength and my Shield, my Fortress and my High Tower. I run to you, Jesus my preserver. I declare and believe that what I am going through today, will bring forth good things in my life as I learn to trust you more. I will glorify you in whatever the seasons may bring.*

Spend some time in praise and worship, continuing to express gratitude toward God. Use the space below for additional journaling or prayer as you feel led.

The end of the matter; all has been heard. Fear God and keep His commandments, for this is the whole duty of man. ~ Ecclesiastes 12:13

The name of the Lord is a strong tower; the righteous man runs
into it and is safe. ~ Proverbs 18:10

Trusting God for Tomorrow

As we look ahead to the future, uncertainty can drift over our hearts. Thoughts of *'What if?'* can make us anxious, especially in areas where we feel limited or out of control. Finances, health, relationships… these are real concerns that can weigh heavily on our minds.

Yet, *you are a daughter of the King*, and He is watching over you. Take a moment to reflect on how *He cares for the lilies of the field and the sparrows in the sky.*

The lilies do not toil, yet they are clothed in splendor. The sparrows do not worry, yet they are fed daily. *How much more will your heavenly Father take care of you?* You are of far greater worth than these, and His love for you is limitless.

Today, take a deep breath and release your worries. *God's provision is sure, His faithfulness is unshakable, and His love for you is endless.* He has not failed you before, and He will not fail you now.

Do not be anxious about anything, but in every situation, by prayer and petition, with thanksgiving, present your requests to God. ~ Philippians 4:6

Journal & Reflection

1. **What areas of your life are you feeling anxious about right now?** Write them down and surrender them to God.

2. **How can you apply the lesson of the lilies and sparrows to your life today?** What would it look like to replace fear with faith?

3. **Can you recall a time when you doubted whether God would provide for you?** How did He come through?

4. **List three prayers that God has answered for you.** Let this be a reminder of His faithfulness.

5. **If you fully trusted in God's provision, how would that change the way you think, act, or pray?**

And my God will meet all your needs according to the riches of his glory in Christ Jesus. ~ Philippians 4:19

Sister, Let today be a day of trust. Rest in the truth that **your future is secure in His hands***.*

Prayer: *Lord help me believe in your great love for me. Help me trust that you will supply all I need, just as you provide for the lilies in the field. Help me see that I am of great value in your eyes. Help me to know you as Jehovah Jirah, the limitless God that provides. Build my faith concerning my future and help me trust as I cast my cares upon you.*

Spend some time in praise and worship, continuing to express gratitude toward God. Use the space below for additional journaling or prayer as you feel led.

Do not be anxious about anything, but in every situation, by prayer and petition, with thanksgiving, present your requests to God. ~ Philippians 4:6

The Lord is my Shephard; I shall not want. ~ Psalm 23:1

Trusting Brings Rest

Victoria Bennett

Be still. Stop striving. Take a rest. Don't that have such a ring to it? There are many days I'd love to have just one extra hour for a power nap. Other days, I had all the extra time in the world, and I would not have described my time as restful.

Discovering the truth that God loves me forever and nothing I can do will change that freed me from the lies that bound me in fear and a works mindset. Torment created a storm in my head that I believed to be "normal". This mindset left a constant whirlwind in my head and heart that never made room for rest.

Truly taking God at His word and believing His promises is what I learned keeps me at rest, despite whatever unknown I may face. In Matthew 8, Jesus was asleep, resting, in the middle of a storm. Chaos was whirling around Him, yet He remained in perfect peace. When His disciples were panicked and woke Him up, Jesus responded by asking them, "Why do you have so little faith?" True rest is trusting God in any storm and every season.

Surrender your anxiety. Be still and realize that I am God. I am God above all the nations, and I am exalted throughout the whole earth. ~ Psalms 46:10 TPT

Journal & Reflection

1. Take a moment to breathe. Breath in God's peace, love, and grace. When you exhale, allow all the stress, business, and worries to leave. Reflect on Psalm 46:10 as you breathe. Ask Holy Spirit what He wants to show you. Journal any thoughts that come to mind as you do this.

For it is by grace you have been saved, through faith—and this is not from yourselves, it is the gift of God— not by works, so that no one can boast. ~ Ephesians 2:8-9

2. What does rest mean to you? What would it look like for you to live from a place of rest and trusting God? How does it reflect your faith?

3. In what ways have you started to doubt God's words? Find what the Word says to be true about those particular areas and write them out. Speak the truth out loud over the lies you have been believing.

4. Is there a place you can imagine that you can go with Jesus, and you would have perfect peace? Journal that place and what the conversation on rest would be between you two.

"Come to me, all you who are weary and burdened, and I will give you rest." ~ Matthew 11:28

Cast all your anxiety on Him because he cares for you.
~ 1 Peter 5:7

We've Got His Power

Anytime we talk, we are speaking life or death in every word. We will see results from what we allow out of our mouths. Our mouth is like a rudder on a boat. Whatever we speak, that's where our life will follow. The enemy gets us to shift our focus on our circumstances instead of keeping them on God, the answer for all things. We glorify the problem instead of the Problem Solver! Then, we incorrectly base our ability to come out of the storm we face on our own strength.

We must arise, ladies!

Let's steer our lives again by speaking what God says! We won't be discouraged! God is faithful to keep His Word. Jesus said in Matthew 17 that if we have faith the size of a mustard seed, we can speak to a mountain and it will move. We know this is because of *who* our faith is in! Let's put our faith back into God's promises and take back the authority we were given and watch God show up and show out on our behalf!

Death and life are in the power of the tongue, and those who love it and indulge it will eat its fruit and bear the consequences of their words. ~ Proverbs 18:21 AMP

Journal & Reflection

1. Would you say that you speak life or death more in your everyday conversations? Be honest with yourself here. Hard conversations with ourselves and God have the potential to bring much-needed change to see the victory we so long for.

2. What area(s) is God showing you that you have been speaking death over? What areas have you been doing a great job at speaking life?

3. Luke 6:45 says, "out of the abundance of the heart the mouth speaks." Often our hearts start to get hardened because of the trials of life. Are there any areas where you have hardened your heart towards God? Ask God to help illuminate those areas and bring healing and truth again.

Look at ships as well: even though they're very big and are driven along by strong winds, they're steered by a very small rudder in the direction the pilot wants to go...

4. I need accountability partners to help me in changing my speech from death to life. I asked my husband and close friends to make me aware when they hear me speaking death. I often become their accountability partner as well. Who can you have this conversation with that can hold you accountable? Journal about what the conversation would be, based on your study of this scripture verse.

...In just the same way the tongue is a very small part of the body, but it makes great boasts! Think how a big forest can be set on fire by a very small flame! ~ James 3:4-5 FBV

Look at ships as well: even though they're very big and are driven along by strong winds, they're steered by a very small rudder in the direction the pilot wants to go. . .

Faith to Prophesy

If you have ever faced a trial that seemed hopeless, then you know the discouragement that can come in the waiting. Often, we give up on God and just accept that this is just the way things will be. God asked Ezekiel, "Can these bones live?" God knew the answer, but He wanted to see what Ezekiel believed. God proceeded by telling him to tell the dry bones to "hear the Word of the Lord!" God then promised to bring breath and life back to the dry bones.

I'm guilty of settling for pain that has resulted from the neck injury I received years ago. I've begun speaking to my neck muscles and telling them to hear the Word of the Lord! I can testify that I've truly seen the "dead valley of dry bones" begin to shake and rattle. Pain I believed came with no ending date has started to cease, as I have been prophesying in faith!

He asked me, "Son of man, can these bones live?" I said, "Sovereign Lord, you alone know." Then he said to me, "Prophesy to these bones and say to them,...

Journal & Reflection

1. Read Ezekiel 37. What phrases or verses stand out ?

2. List out your "dry bones", the trials that have gone on for a long time with no hope in sight.

3. Often we miss what God is doing in the small things because we look for the major things. Take this time to ponder on the small progress you have missed in relation to the "dry bones" listed above. Thank Him for all that He has done in those areas.

. . . 'Dry bones, hear the word of the Lord! This is what the Sovereign Lord says to these bones: I will make breath enter you, and you will come to life I will attach tendons to you . . .

4. It takes great faith to prophesy to a bunch of dead, dry bones. Mathew 17:20 says, "Faith the size of a mustard seed can move a mountain.". Write out what mustard seed faith you have for the "dry bones" in your life. In what places can you hear a rattling?

5. Here is the fun part! Open your mouth and prophesy to each "dry bone" and tell them to "hear the Word of the Lord!" They will live again, and hope will begin to be restored in you as you speak. Come back to this space as you begin to see the valley of dry bones start to come to life!

. . .and make flesh come upon you and cover you with skin; I will put breath in you, and you will come to life. Then you will know that I am the Lord."' ~ Ezekiel 37:3-6

When he had said these things, he cried out with a loud voice,
"Lazarus, come out." The man who had died came out...
~ John 11:43-44

A Faith-Filled Oasis

Renee Kelley

Faith and trust are intimately tied together with our relationship with God.

When you learn to trust the Lord with the very air you breathe and with all that you hold dear, that is when you will find true peace. Learn to lean more on the Lord Jesus Christ and lean not to your own understanding and he will guide you through all that life has in store.

Let Him become your True Oasis!

It is the greatest challenge that brings the best reward when you allow the Peace of God to rule your heart.

And let the peace of God rule in your hearts, to the which also ye are called in one body; and be ye thankful.

~ Colossians 3:15 (KJV)

Journal & Reflection

Do you find yourself not having peace during the midst of your storms?

What are three things you could change today, that would allow God's Peace to rule?

1.

2.

3.

Are you very busy and have a hard time setting aside adequate time for prayer and the reading of God's Word?

What are three changes you could make in your schedule to give Him a little more time?

1.

2.

3.

You keep him in perfect peace whose mind is stayed on you, because he trusts in you. ~ Isaiah 26:3

How Do You Find Your Oasis?

It is a powerful revelation when we realize we can do all things because of God's strength. When I was going through some of the most difficult trials in my life, God helped me to shed away the fear of man and just to focus on Him and His presence no matter where I was. This created an Oasis for me in a time when I felt like I was walking through the desert.

He can do the same for you too!

Focus on Him. Enter into His courts with praise, thanksgiving, and songs of worship. Let Him fight the battle for you. You need only to drink from the living waters of your Oasis in Him.

I can do all things through Christ who strengthens me.
~ Philippians 4:13

Journal & Reflection

Do you feel that you are tired and often weak and do not have the strength to carry on?

Are there three things that you could speak over yourself that would change the way you view yourself? Write them here.

1.

2.

3.

Are there three scriptures you could research and stand on that would change your view of your circumstances?

1.

2.

3.

But they who wait for the Lord shall renew their strength; they shall mount up with wings like eagles; they shall run and not be weary; they shall walk and not faint. ~ Isaiah 40:31

How to Remain in the Oasis by Faith

When trouble comes your way, and it will come, can you look beyond it all and realize God will turn things around for your good?

Often in the midst of trials, it's easy to feel as though God has abandoned us or doesn't see what we're going through. But that is far from the truth. He has promised He will never leave us nor forsake us. He is with us in the storms of life.

He does call us higher to a place of surrender and trust. It requires saying, "Thy will be done," and choosing to follow Him no matter what.

And we know that all things work together for good to them that love God, to them who are the called according to His purpose.

~ Romans 8:28 (KJV)

Can you think of three things that will help you see you are never alone?

1.

2.

3.

Do you trust the Lord no matter what?

Is there something you are holding on to, something you think is really too hard for God?

Can you think of at least three things you have not been able to release into his mighty hands?

1.

2.

3

Take a moment to just write down what changes you can make today, that will forge the way to your Oasis.

It is the Lord who goes before you. He will be with you; He will not leave you or forsake you. Do not fear or be dismayed.
~ Joshua 31:8

Walking As a New Creation

Dawn Anderson

When your relationship was established with the Lord Jesus Christ, the old is gone and the new was created. We were created in His likeness and God doesn't see the old person anymore. This is our opportunity daily to walk in that. We must put off the old and put on the new by faith. Why would we carry a dead person around on our back when God already buried that person? God only sees us as new and invites us to view ourselves the same way!

"...and to put on the new self, which in the likeness of God has been created in righteousness and holiness of the truth." ~ Ephesians 4:24

What does this verse say about who you are? What words stand out that you can claim about you in Christ?

I have been crucified with Christ. It is no longer I who live, but Christ who lives in me. And the life I now live...

"...and have put on the new self, which is being renewed to a true
knowledge according to the image of the One who created it..."
~ Colossians 3:10

What are some I AM statements that you get from these verses?

Therefore if anyone is in Christ, this person is a new creation; the old
things passed away; behold, new things have come.
~ 2 Corinthians 5:17

What true knowledge has the Lord provided you about how He perfected
you?

What is a daily reminder you can write to remind yourself to let go of the
old things are gone and God has all new things prepared for you?

...in the flesh I live by faith in the Son of God, who loved me
and gave himself for me. ~ Galatians 2:20

Own Your Inheritance

Not only are you a new creation you were given an inheritance at the moment you believed! Part of the family of God. Nothing we can do can remove that birthright! As a daughter of the King how would you walk, and talk knowing you are an heir to his throne? How would that impact your faith and the prayers that you pray? Would you talk about who your Father is? Would your awareness about how you speak even of yourself change? What do you believe the Lord says about you? The power of God's Word and the sound of your own voice is the most powerful voice you hear!

For you are all sons and daughters of God
through faith in Christ Jesus. ~ Galatians 3:26

What does God tell you here about how He receives you?

For you did not receive the spirit of slavery to fall back into fear, but you have received the Spirit of adoption as sons, by whom we cry, "Abba! Father!" The Spirit himself bears witness with our spirit...

But I say, walk by the Spirit, and you will not carry out the desire of the flesh. ~ Galatians 5:16

What power do you know have to live in the new creation as a daughter of the King?

Righteous lips are the delight of kings, and one who speaks right is loved. ~ Proverbs 16:13

How can you utilize the power you have in the words you speak? What does God tell you in this verse about how He receives you?

that we are children of God, and if children, then heirs—heirs of God and fellow heirs with Christ, provided we suffer with him in order that we may also be glorified with him.
~ Romans 8:15-17

You Were Designed ON PURPOSE, WITH A PURPOSE, *and* FOR A PURPOSE!

❧

He is always ready and available for us. Taking the time to talk to Him and more importantly listen to what He wants to tell us is where we glean wisdom. The Lord has no desire to hold anything good back from us. He gives us instruction in His Word and through our prayer time with Him. Are you searching for more of what the Lord has for you? Do you spend time in gratitude for the inheritance you have already received? Do you believe these things are true: that He wants to listen and answer you and to spend time with you and direct you?

❧

"Call to Me and I will answer you, and I will tell you great and mighty things, which you do not know." ~ Jeremiah 33:3

What do you have to do to get God's attention?

You will seek me and find me, when you seek me with all your heart. ~ Jeremiah 29:13

Commit your works to the Lord, and your plans will be established.
~ Proverbs 16:3

How will the Lord guide and direct you according to this verse?

One who gets wisdom loves his own soul; one who keeps understanding
will find good. ~ Proverbs 19:8

When we seek God's wisdom what do we receive?

. . . the Lord will continually guide you,
And satisfy your desire in scorched places,
And give strength to your bones;
And you will be like a watered garden,
And like a spring of water whose waters do not fail.
~ Isaiah 58:11

As the Lord guides us, we are watered like a garden, and what comes from that water?

Behold, you delight in truth in the inward being, and you teach
me wisdom in the secret heart. ~ Psalm 51:6

But if any of you lacks wisdom, let him ask of God, who gives to all generously and without reproach, and it will be given to him.
~ James 1:5

What do we need to do to receive wisdom from the Lord? How much does He promise to give? What type of a response do we get from God when we go to him and ask?

Give thanks to the Lord of lords, for His faithfulness is everlasting. ~ Psalms 136:3

The Lord is FAITHFUL!
In response we are to be grateful. How many things has He shown you through these last journal days that we can be grateful for? List them and add more to the list daily!

For great is His steadfast love toward us, and the faithfulness of the Lord endures forever. Praise the Lord! ~ Psalm 117:2

Prayer:: *Thank you, Lord, that we are a new creation in you! Thank you for the generous wisdom you promise us and the direction you have for our lives. We are grateful that you are FAITHFUL in all our circumstances. In Jesus' Name, Amen.*

Use the space for additional journaling and reflecting on the Lord's faithfulness in your life.

All the paths of the Lord are steadfast love and faithfulness, for those who keep his covenant and his testimonies.

~ Psalm 25:10

Wisdom for the Journey

Shontal LeJune

✿❀✿

It takes great faith to navigate a healing journey, and seeking wisdom and inviting God into that journey is a cornerstone of walking through it in faith. It is important to dedicate yourself to learning, even when it's difficult or costly. This pursuit shapes your entire life, not just healing. Having humility and trusting the process for your health influences your healing and can bring you to higher levels of faith, peace and strength. Let this be a reflection on surrendering control and embracing God's direction and will for your life.

When you seek wisdom, you are not walking this journey alone. God, the giver of all understanding, is leading and protecting you. Even when the path feels uncertain, He shields those who trust Him. If you are in a season of searching—whether for healing, purpose, or clarity—have faith that He is guiding your steps. Trust that His wisdom will light your way, and His faithfulness will sustain you. Keep walking forward, for He has already prepared the way ahead.

For the Lord gives wisdom; From His mouth come knowledge and understanding. He stores up sound wisdom for the upright; He is a shield to those who walk in integrity...

Journal & Reflection

Seeking Divine Wisdom

In what areas of your life do you need greater wisdom and discernment?

How can you intentionally invite God's guidance into your decisions, trusting that His wisdom will lead you even when the path ahead is uncertain?

Surrendering Control

What fears or struggles make it difficult for you to fully surrender to God's plan?

How can you practice releasing control and embracing His wisdom, knowing that true healing—physically, emotionally, and spiritually—comes through trust in Him?

...Guarding the paths of justice, And He watches over the way of His godly ones. ~ Proverbs 2:6-8 (NASB)

Recognizing Growth & Purpose

Reflecting on past challenges, what key insights has God revealed to you?

How have those lessons shaped your faith, and how can they strengthen your confidence in His plan for your future?

For the Lord gives wisdom; From His mouth come knowledge and understanding. He stores up sound wisdom for the upright; He is a shield to those who walk in integrity...

. . . Guarding the paths of justice, And He watches over the way of His godly ones. ~ Proverbs 2:6-8 (NASB)

Inviting God Into
Your Healing Journey

Healing is a journey of seeking deeper understanding—of yourself, your body, and the wisdom God provides. Along the way, challenges arise, requiring shifts in mindset, lifestyle, and faith. True transformation is rarely immediate; it unfolds through persistence, surrender, and the willingness to grow. Wisdom, like healing, is a process—one that refines, strengthens, and brings clarity over time.

As you navigate this season, lean into the lessons emerging from your struggles. Trust that even in uncertainty, God is guiding you, equipping you with the insight needed to move forward. Each step, no matter how small, is shaping you for something greater. Embrace the unfolding, knowing that growth and renewal are already at work within you.

The beginning of wisdom is: Acquire wisdom; And with all your possessions, acquire understanding. ~ Proverbs 4:7 (NASB)

Journal & Reflection

Lessons for Struggle

Consider a time when you received clarity or insight after a period of struggle. How did that wisdom change the course of your journey?

Faith in the Process

Think about the role of faith in your current season. How can you strengthen your trust in God as you move forward with Him?

Seeking Wisdom in Healing

What areas of your health journey require greater wisdom?

How can you cultivate and pursue deeper understanding, despite the challenges?

Look at ships as well: even though they're very big and are driven along by strong winds, they're steered by a very small rudder in the direction the pilot wants to go...

Humility and Trust in the Process

Healing is not just about the physical, emotional, or spiritual aspects of life—it's about aligning every part of you with God's wisdom. As you journey through this season, take comfort in knowing that God's guidance will lead you to peace, inner strength, and a renewed sense of purpose.

When you surrender control and trust His process, He will reveal a path of restoration. Even when the way seems unclear, remember that His wisdom brings clarity, and His presence offers peace, and strengthens your faith as you move forward with confidence and hope.

Do not be wise in your own eyes; Fear the Lord and turn away from evil. It will be healing to your body And refreshment to your bones. ~ Proverbs 3:7-8 (NASB)

Journal & Reflection

Trusting God's Will

How can you trust in God's healing power and wisdom to guide you through your current struggles, and what steps can you take today to align your life with His divine plan?

Strengthening Faith Through Peace

Reflecting on a time when you experienced God's peace, how can that moment strengthen your faith and shape your journey moving forward?

Humility and Surrender in Healing

How does cultivating humility and surrendering control to God impact your physical, emotional, and spiritual healing, and how can you embrace His wisdom to walk confidently into tomorrow?

Look at ships as well: even though they're very big and are driven along by strong winds, they're steered by a very small rudder in the direction the pilot wants to go. . .

Faith to Move Mountains

Lesa Dale

✻✻

How often do we limit God—not just in what we ask, but in what we think He can do? Do we truly grasp the power at work within us? We hesitate to ask for miracles, believe in healing, and expect the supernatural as if God is bound by our limitations. But He is eternal. His power is not subject to time, doubt, or human reasoning. What if we dared to believe bigger? What if we removed the boundaries of our own understanding and let faith rise to match the immeasurable greatness of our God?

✻✻

1. Are there areas where you have unknowingly limited what God can do?

"Now to him who is able to do immeasurably more than all we ask or imagine, according to his power that is at work within us." ~ Ephesians 3:20 (NIV)

2. What have you avoided asking God for because it seems too big or impossible?

3. How would your faith change if you truly believed God's power is at work within you?

4. What miracles do you see in Scripture that you struggle to believe could happen today?

5. How can you expand your faith and imagination to align with the fullness of God's power?

Jesus replied, "Truly I tell you, if you have faith and do not doubt, not only can you do what was done to the fig tree, but also you can say to this mountain, 'Go, throw yourself into the sea,' and it will be done. If you believe, you will receive whatever you ask for in prayer." ~ Matthew 21:21-22 (NIV)

Prayer: *Father, forgive me for the times I have made You small in my mind. You are not limited by time, my understanding, or human reasoning. You can do immeasurably more than I could ever ask or imagine. Increase my faith, Lord. Help me to believe in the impossible, to trust in Your supernatural power, and to walk in the fullness of what You have given me. Let my life reflect the limitless nature of Your glory. In Jesus' name, Amen.*

Use the space below for additional reflection and journaling as needed.

"Now to him who is able to do immeasurably more than all we ask or imagine, according to his power that is at work within us." ~ Ephesians 3:20 (NIV)

Jesus replied, "Truly I tell you, if you have faith and do not doubt,
not only can you do what was done to the fig tree, but also you can say
to this mountain, 'Go, throw yourself into the sea,' and it will be done.
If you believe, you will receive whatever you ask for in prayer." ~
Matthew 21:21-22 (NIV)

Faith to Forgive Fully

Forgiveness is not optional—it is expected. Jesus has entrusted us with forgiving sin, just as He has forgiven us. Forgiveness is more than letting go of hurt feelings or offenses; it actively releases people from the weight of their wrongdoing. When we withhold forgiveness, we keep others in bondage—not just in our hearts but in the spiritual realm as well.

God's grace does not flow selectively. He doesn't forgive us while allowing us to remain bitter toward others. His forgiveness changes us and calls us to do the same for others. Choosing to forgive doesn't mean saying that sin doesn't matter. It means declaring that God's mercy is more. If we genuinely know that Jesus' sacrifice was enough for us, we must also believe it is enough for others.

Forgiveness is an act of obedience. It is surrendering our right to hold onto pain and demand payment for the wrongs done against us. And in that surrender, we find freedom—not just for them, but for ourselves.

1. Have you ever struggled with forgiving someone because you felt they didn't deserve it?

"If you forgive anyone's sins, their sins are forgiven; if you do not forgive them, they are not forgiven."
~ John 20:23 (NIV)

2. How does knowing that forgiveness is a divine expectation change your perspective?

3. What burdens are you carrying because of withheld forgiveness?

4. How does your understanding of God's grace shape how you extend forgiveness to others?

5. Who do you need to forgive today—not just in word, but in spirit?

Prayer: *Father, I acknowledge that forgiveness is not just something I receive—it is something You expect me to give. You have forgiven me completely, and I am called to do the same for others. Help me to release the weight of bitterness, to surrender my need for justice, and to trust You with the outcome. Let my life reflect Your mercy. May I be an instrument of Your grace, extending forgiveness as freely as I have received it? In Jesus' name, Amen.*

"For if you forgive others when they sin against you, your heavenly Father will also forgive you. But if you do not forgive others their sins, your Father will not forgive your sins." ~
Matthew 6:14-15 (NIV)

Faith to Boldly Approach His Throne

Jabez *asked*—not timidly, but with confidence in the God who keeps His promises. His prayer wasn't just wishful thinking; it was rooted in knowing that God is faithful to bless those who call on Him. Throughout Scripture, we see God inviting His people to ask, seek, and knock (Matthew 7:7-8). He tells us to approach Him boldly (Hebrews 4:16) because He has already promised to supply our needs, to guide us, and to give us good things (Philippians 4:19, Psalm 84:11).

Yet, how often do we hesitate? Do we hold back from asking because we feel unworthy or don't believe God wants to bless us? The truth is, God's blessings are never just about us—they are meant to *flow through* us to others. When we pray for more, we ask for more impact, opportunities to serve, and alignment with His purpose. God is not reluctant to bless us; He is waiting for us to trust Him enough to ask.

"Jabez cried out to the God of Israel, 'Oh, that You would bless me and enlarge my territory! Let Your hand be with me and keep me from harm so I will be free from pain.' And God granted his request." ~ 1 Chronicles 4:10 (NIV)

1. What promises of God can you stand on when you pray boldly for His blessing?

2. Do you hesitate to ask for more? If so, what holds you back?

3. How does understanding God's faithfulness and promises change the way you pray?

4. What areas of your life do you need God to "enlarge"—your faith, your influence, your capacity to serve?

5. How can you position yourself as a vessel through which God's blessings flow to others?

"Ask and it will be given to you; seek and you will find; knock and the door will be opened to you. For everyone who asks receives; the one who seeks finds; and to the one who knocks, the door will be opened." ~ Matthew 7:7-8 (NIV)

Prayer: *Father, You are a promise-keeping God, and today, I come before You in faith. You have invited me to ask, and I take You at Your word. Bless me, Lord— not just for my sake, but so that I can bless others. Enlarge my territory, increase my capacity to serve, and let Your promises be fulfilled. Remove any hesitation or doubt that keeps me from seeking more of You. I trust in Your faithfulness and receive all You have for me. In Jesus' name, Amen.*

Use the space below for additional prayers, journaling, and reflection.

For the Lord God is a sun and shield;
the Lord bestows favor and honor. ~ Psalm 84:11

Let us then with confidence draw near to the throne of grace, that we may receive mercy and find grace to help in time of need. ~ Hebrews 4:16

The Princess

Melissa Eiserer

❦

Consider the attitude of a Proverbs 31 woman and how she is much like a princess; she is a faithful servant to those around her. She is praised for her faith!

Circle the things, about yourself, that you believe you are doing well as a servant of God. Are you:

Noble

Worthy

Dignified

Strong

Strong and Healthy

Vigorous/a Willing Worker

a Preparer of Healthy Food

A Good Model of Work

Giving to Those in Need

Clothing Your Family Well

Heart Ready for God's Use

Praiseworthy

Someone Who Adds Value

Praised by Your Husband

a Woman Who Fears the Lord

Speaking with Wisdom

Respected

Confident

Stewarding Well Your Money

Instructing Faithfully

Frugal

Called Blessed by Your Children and Husband

Charm is deceitful and beauty is passing, but a woman who fears the Lord, she shall be praised. Give her of the fruit of her hands, and let her own works praise her in the gates.
~ Proverbs 31:30-31

In what ways do you personally feel you show up "dressed and ready," happy and willing as a princess-servant of God?

In the following space take time to write a prayer based off the scripture at the bottom of this page and of thanksgiving for the things you circled above:

Be dressed and ready for service and keep your lamps burning ~
Luke 12:35

The Warrior Bride

Now consider the attitude of a Proverbs 31 woman as a warrior—especially when it feels like you are lacking the faithfulness to serve others, or you find it hard to pull the strength from within.

Circle the things you believe you could be better at as a servant of God.

Are you being:

Noble

Worthy

Dignified

Strong

Strong and Healthy

Vigorous/a Willing Worker

a Preparer of Healthy Food

A Good Model of Work

Giving to Those in Need

Clothing Your Family Well

Heart Ready for God's Use

Someone Who Adds Value

Praiseworthy

Praised by Your Husband

a Woman Who Fears the Lord

Speaking with Wisdom

Respected

Confident

Instructing Faithfully

Stewarding Well Your Money

Frugal

Called Blessed by Your Children and Husband

I can do all things through Christ who strengthens me
~ Philippians 4:13

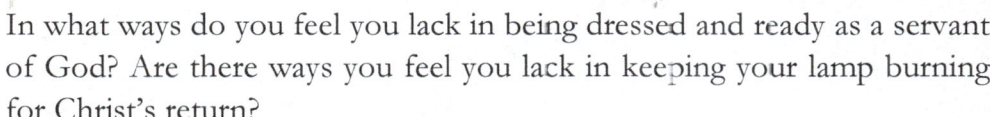

In what ways do you feel you lack in being dressed and ready as a servant of God? Are there ways you feel you lack in keeping your lamp burning for Christ's return?

What do you think steals your strength in Christ?

What do you think you can do differently to become the Proverbs 31 Woman Warrior for God you want to be?

And the Lord shall help and deliver them; He shall deliver them from the wicked and save them because they trust in Him ~

Psalm 37:40

A Proverbs 31 Armored Woman of God

As a Proverbs 31 woman, you work as a daughter of God and a faithful warrior, but what must you do to protect the work you do?

Consider how the actions you take demonstrate your faith and help it to grow!

Circle the things you do often to protect your spiritual self:

Bible Study	Journaling	Prayer Time
Spa Day	Retreats	Conferences
Christian Music	Reading	Devotionals
Sessions with your Pastor/Counselor	Church	Self-Improvement Books

What is one thing you would like to add/do to help you keep your lamp burning for Christ's return?

Write down a Month, Day, and Year you are going to do it:

After reading the scripture below, write a prayer for yourself—yes, yourself! You may even want to copy it to a notecard and keep it in your bible, journal, or purse; somewhere that you can access it every day to read often.

Finally, be strong in the Lord and in the strength of His might.
Put on the full armor of God, so that you will be able to stand firm against the schemes of the devil.
For our struggle is not against flesh and blood, but against the rulers, against the powers, against the world forces of this darkness, against the spiritual forces of wickedness in the heavenly places.
Therefore, take up the full armor of God, so that you will be able to resist in the evil day, and having done everything, to stand firm.
Stand firm therefore, having girded your loins with truth, and having put on the breastplate of righteousness,
And having shod your feet with the preparation of the gospel of peace.
In addition to all, taking up the shield of faith with which you will be able to extinguish all the flaming arrows of the evil one.
And take the helmet of salvation, and the sword of the Spirit, which is the work of God.
With all prayer and petition pray at all times in the Spirit, and with this in view, be on the alert with all perseverance and petition for all the saints, And Pray. ~ Ephesians 6:10-19

An excellent wife who can find? She is far more precious than jewels. ~ Proverbs 31:10

For the weapons of our warfare are not carnal but mighty in God for pulling down strongholds ~ 2 Corinthians 10:4

Faith to Surrender

Katelyn Silva

It takes great faith to wholly surrender to God in all things. It's much easier to worry, to go over possible outcomes or current circumstances over and over in your mind, and to try to conceive how you will react or handle each one. Instead, we are encouraged to do the opposite: surrender all things to the Lord and receive His peace regardless of circumstances.

In what ways are you currently experiencing worry, anxiety, uncertainty, fears or burdens?

...do not be anxious about anything, but in everything by prayer and supplication with thanksgiving let your requests be made known to God...

What prevents you from truly opening your hands and laying these things at the Lord's feet?

Consider the Lord's faithfulness. Journal and thank Him for the ways He has already worked, provided, and answered prayers throughout your life.

Write a prayer to the Lord of surrender. Continue from this prompt or write your own:

Heavenly Father, thank you that you are my Good Shephard and that you care for even my smallest struggles. Help me to surrender more fully and to lay down my worries at your feet and receive your peace in exchange...

. . . and the peace of God, which surpasses all understanding, will guard your hearts and your minds in Christ Jesus."

~ Philippians 4:6-7

Faith to Be Full of the Holy Spirit

I once heard a pastor say, "If it hurts, you haven't really died." *'What?! That seems extreme. Life is full of hurt.'* But the pastor went on to explain that he meant the death of self, of pride, of worldly ambition. How easy it is to fix our minds and intentions on things of this world and then tell ourselves it's really for the Kingdom. How easy to do what is comfortable or convenient and miss out on the glory God has for today, or to become offended by what someone says and want to defend ourselves.

What if instead, by faith, we really believed and lived out what Jesus said: that God will provide for our every need, every day; that we can store up Heavenly treasure and reward through our kind service toward others; that we can move mountains and do greater works than He did! When Peter was focused on the world, he denied Christ three times. When Peter was humbled, had truly died to self, and was full of the Holy Spirit, he spoke with boldness and thousands were saved and miracles followed him. Use these prompts to consider whether you've died to self and to the world so that the Holy Spirit can live through you, and you can live with eternity in mind.

"If then you have been raised with Christ, seek the things that are above, where Christ is, seated at the right hand of God. . .

Have you ever felt the nudge of the Holy Spirit to pray for someone or witness to someone, but you held back because of fear, pride, or doubt? Have you ever felt that nudge and listened? What were the outcomes of each situation?

Have you witnessed or experienced someone or yourself being full of the Holy Spirit? If so, describe the experience. If not, do you believe you can be? Do a word study on "full of the Holy Spirit" and write what you find.

Consider honestly the fruit of your life so far. Does it reflect a focus on eternity or have the worries of the world crept in? Journal with the Lord about this.

Prayer: *Lord Jesus, purify me as fire and cleanse me of anything that does not please you. Baptize me in and fill me with your Holy Spirit so that I may speak with boldness, obey your voice daily, and live for eternal things. Re-ignite my fire for you and give me your faith. Amen.*

. . . Set your minds on things that are above, not on things that are on earth. For you have died, and your life is hidden with Christ in God." ~ Colossians 3:1-3

Faith to Wait on the Lord

I believe that waiting on the Lord often takes some of the greatest faith, perhaps even greater than faith for miracles. After all, faith is evidence of things not seen (Hebrews 11:1) yet trusting God to bring those things to pass. There are many examples of men in the Bible who lived this, and one I often consider is Joseph. His circumstances seemed to be the exact opposite of what God had revealed to him. By the world's standards, he had every reason to doubt, to rely on his own understanding, and to even deny God. But he didn't. He fled temptation. He glorified God always. He trusted God in every circumstance, and the Lord did indeed direct his paths, right into the Pharoah's court and a position to save nations.

Has the Lord placed a dream in your heart or given you a confirmation that the answer to your prayers will come, yet you have been waiting and wondering *when*? In what ways could the Lord be preparing you or training you?

Trust in the Lord with all your heart, and lean not on your own understanding . . .

What do you believe fully trusting God looks like? How can you live that out more fully?

How have you been leaning on your own understanding?

Do a brief study on the phrase "wait on the Lord" in the Bible. How can this strengthen your faith? Journal your findings.

Prayer: *Heavenly Father, thank you for your sovereignty and your wisdom. Thank you that your ways and thoughts are higher and that I can trust in you completely. Make me like Joseph, and help me to trust you with all my heart, knowing you direct my paths and work all things for good and conform me to the image of your Son. Amen.*

. . .in all your ways acknowledge Him, and He shall direct your paths. ~ Proverbs 3:5-6

Additional Journaling Space

For by grace you have been saved through faith, and that not of yourselves; it is the gift of God not of works, lest anyone should boast...

Additional Journaling Space

. . . For we are His workmanship, created in Christ Jesus for good works, which God prepared beforehand that we should walk in them. ~ Ephesians 2:9-10

Additional Journaling Space

May the God of hope fill you with all joy and peace as you trust in him, so that you may overflow with hope by the power of the Holy Spirit. ~ Romans 15:13

About the Authors

Jill Albanys

Jill is a Kingdom-minded Life and Business Coach dedicated to helping women step boldly into their God-given calling as coaches, ministers, and speakers. With a deep passion for freedom and joy, she empowers women to break through financial and spiritual limitations so they can impact lives through coaching, writing, and speaking. Beyond coaching, Jill serves as an assistant pastor and worship leader, using her voice to inspire and uplift. Having walked through both poverty and abundance, she understands the power of transformation and is committed to equipping women for a life of financial freedom—allowing them to spend more time doing what they love with the people they love. Connect with Jill at: facebook.com/jill.albanys.

Dawn Anderson

Dawn Anderson is a powerhouse who has walked through much adversity and come out a conqueror. She is a single mom of eight, a bestselling author, a realtor, a highly sought-after speaker, and a success coach. Dawn has spoken to thousands and is passionate about encouraging and empowering others to pursue their passion and live life by design. She teaches others how to "start from within" to make lasting changes. Learn more at: www.DawnAndersonCoaching.com.

Victoria Bennett

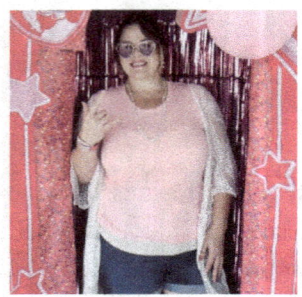

Victoria Bennett is the owner of *Booth #5 – Vintage and Grace* where she displays her various crafts and antiques, with inspiration from her walk with the Holy Spirit. She is passionate about God and sharing hope and encouragement and faith with others through her creative gifts. Learn more at: facebook.com/groups/1103640528152733.

Lesa Dale

Lesa Dale, a lover of the Lord and plain ol' coffee, founded Life Walk GPS, LLC. As a Kingdom Purpose & Alignment Guide, speaker, and author trained in Spiritual Gifts and DISC profiling, she helps Christians move from uncertainty to confidence by discovering God's unique purpose for their lives. Using assessments of gifts, personalities, and strengths, Lesa equips her clients to make life decisions that align with God's plan, allowing them to thrive, become a light to the world doing what lights them up, and create a legacy of abundance. Learn more at www.lesadale.com.

Melissa Eiserer

Melissa Eiserer BSE, MS, Founder and CEO of Melissa Eiserer Career Coaching and Consulting, is a sought-after career and school counselor with 30+ years of experience specializing in personal career coaching, consulting, job preparation, and professional training. She is a faith-based career coach, speaker, and professional, who works with all students and homeschool families to explore career options beyond high school. She guides students to find their best career pathway, minimize higher education debt, and step into a successful future by determining who they want to be and what that might look like. Learn more by connecting on Facebook: www.facebook.com/melissa.eiserer.

Renee Kelley

Renee Kelley is a wife, mother, grandmother (G-Na) author, speaker, minister, life coach, and realtor. Renee is passionate about the things of God. She loves helping others overcome obstacles and challenges. She is self-driven and self-motivated. She is always careful to give God the glory for where she is and what she has come through. Renee enjoys helping clients achieve their hopes, goals, and dreams. She loves inspiring others to greatness, to do better and be better. She encourages all to fulfill their vision of the future. Coach Kelley would love to come along side of you and help you reach your ultimate dreams. Connect with Renee: facebook.com/share/15qbDRbtEL/?mibextid=wwXIfr.

Get Renee's other book, *The Raising of a Prophet*: amazon.com/dp/1541034775.

Shontal LeJune

Shontal LeJune is an Integrative Nutrition Health Coach, certified by the Institute of Integrative Nutrition. Her approach came through her own experience overcoming undiagnosed health issues post-pregnancy, which led to complete transformation through holistic learning and practices. She now helps others also experience health and life transformation through positive, holistic practices and changes. Learn more at www.SunshineLiving.net.

Katelyn Silva

Katelyn Silva is the 6x international bestselling author of thirteen books and counting, some under a pen name. She is a God-fearing devoted wife and home-schooling mother of four. She is the founder of We Write Books, Coffee Date with Jesus, and is the host of the 1 Minute Writing Tip podcast. She works with Holy Spirit-led women to get clarity on their book idea, confidently write and publish a bestseller, and use it as a tool for impact, authority, and accomplishing their God-given purpose. She believes every person has a unique story worth telling and that your book can change a life. Learn more at www.wewritebooks.com.

Continue your faith journey with She Laughs at the Future.

Part of life is experiencing difficult things. There are seasons of joy and seasons of pain. But it's important to remember that these are just that… seasons. They won't last forever. More importantly, you are never alone. God is with you. He sees you. He will carry you through. And He always makes the broken beautiful and uses everything for good.

It's so easy to slip into despair, worry, fear, hopelessness… But God has grace that abounds beyond what you can imagine. And part of rising out of that is through others' testimonies.

That's exactly what you'll find in *She Laughs at the Future*.

This collection of testimonies shares real stories from those who went through some of life's most difficult challenges and yet came out with faith and hope and strength greater than ever. Renew your faith and walk in the joy and peace that allows you to **laugh without fear of the future**.

Get your copy of She Laughs at the Future wherever books are sold.

More From *She Laughs at the Future*

11 oz $12
15 oz $15

$17

$17

11 oz $12
15 oz $15

$17

$16

Get one or more of these beautiful reminders of faith.
Reach out to Jill Albanys for details:
facebook.com/jill.albanys